Our Changing Earth

by Kim Borland

Forces of Change

When you stand on the ground, Earth feels solid beneath your feet. But did you know that our planet is moving and changing all the time? It's true! Although you can't feel it, Earth's rocks are constantly pushing, squeezing, and pulling beneath your feet.

Forces inside Earth and on its surface change Earth's rocks. These forces cause rocks to slowly bend, twist, and turn. Earth's rocks are constantly bending, twisting, and turning.

Some forces change Earth's surface quickly. Those forces include earthquakes and volcanoes. Other forces change Earth's surface very slowly. Those forces include weathering and erosion. Some forces take a very long time to change Earth!

Earth from space

Earth's Layers

Our planet is made up of several layers of rock. Scientists learn about Earth by studying these different layers. Scientists study the layers near Earth's surface. They also study the layers deep under the ground.

The **crust** is the hard, rocky layer that forms Earth's surface. Below the crust is the mantle. The **mantle** is the thickest layer of Earth. It is more than two thousand miles thick. It makes up more than most of Earth's total volume.

Geologists study Earth's crust.

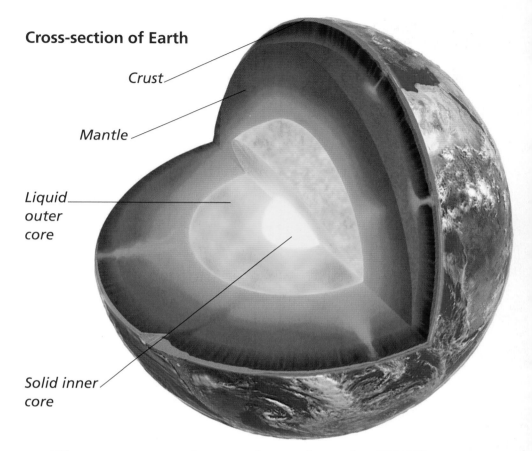

Cross-section of Earth

Crust

Mantle

Liquid
outer
core

Solid inner
core

The innermost layer of Earth is the **core.** It is made mostly of iron and nickel. Iron and nickel are metals. The core has two layers. Those layers are the outer core and the inner core. The outer core is a very hot liquid. At Earth's center is the inner core. It is solid and hard.

Earth is coolest at the crust. It is hottest at the core. Earth's core is about one hundred times hotter than the hottest desert!

Shapes on Earth's Surface

A **landform** is a solid feature formed on Earth's crust. Hills, mountains, valleys, and plains are landforms. Waterfalls, cliffs, islands, and caves are landforms too. Even volcanoes are landforms.

Landforms are of different shapes and sizes. But all landforms are alike in one important way. They are all shaped by natural forces. Those forces include heat, wind, water, and ice.

Desert

Waterfall

Rock butte

Many landforms are shaped by moving water. Rivers carve out valleys as they flow. Sand and small rocks carried in rivers wear away the land. The material that is worn off gets carried away. Then it gets left in new places.

Waves

Volcano

Mountain lake

Volcanoes and Earthquakes

Volcanoes can cause rapid changes to Earth's landscape. They contain **magma.** Magma is hot, molten rock. It sits in pockets called magma chambers. Gases in the magma create pressure. The pressure forces the magma through a central vent. The central vent leads to the top of the volcano.

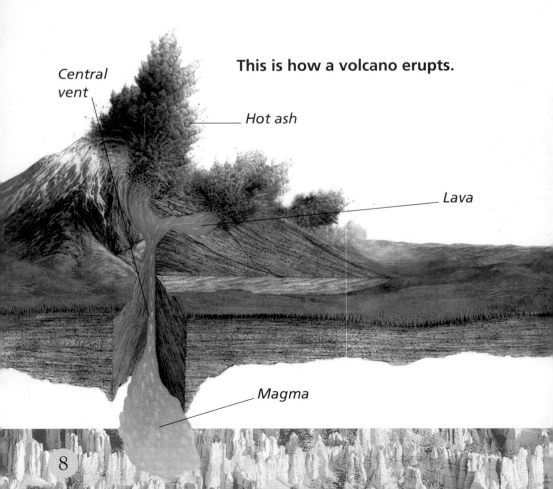

This is how a volcano erupts.

Central vent

Hot ash

Lava

Magma

Ash erupts from Mount St. Helens.

Magma erupts from a vent.

When the magma reaches the volcano's top, the volcano erupts. Sometimes magma erupts through side vents. But it usually erupts through the volcano's top.

Volcanoes send steam, rocks, and ash into the air when they erupt. **Lava** is magma that reaches the surface. It flows down the slopes and burns everything in its path. Lava is eight times hotter than boiling water! When lava cools, it becomes hard, igneous rock. That rock is a new part of Earth's crust.

California's San Andreas Fault is more than eight hundred miles long.

Earthquakes

An earthquake is a natural force that shakes the ground. Earthquakes happen when pieces of Earth's crust rub together along faults, or cracks.

Earthquakes produce waves of vibrations. These waves move up and down and back and forth.

1906 San Francisco earthquake

Earthquake Damage

Powerful earthquakes can cause a lot of damage. Earthquakes that are closer to the surface cause more damage. The longer an earthquake lasts, the more damage it can cause. The nearer an earthquake is to a city, the more buildings will be damaged.

Earthquakes cause landslides, which also cause damage. Landslides are rocks and soil that slide down the side of a hill. They can destroy buildings and roads. Landslides also happen in the ocean. There they can create huge, dangerous waves.

Weathering

You may not see weathering happen. But weathering goes on all the time. **Weathering** is a process that breaks down rocks on Earth's surface into smaller and smaller pieces. Plants, animals, insects, and other living things can cause weathering. Water, wind, and ice can cause weathering too. Sometimes weathering changes only take a few years. Other times they take centuries.

Plants are just one cause of weathering. Plants cause weathering by forcing their roots into cracks in rocks. As the roots grow, they split the rocks.

Snow-capped mountains

Glaciers

Water causes weathering too. Sometimes water picks up special chemicals from soil. The chemicals eat away at rocks the water touches. This is called chemical weathering.

Ice also weathers rocks. Water can get into cracks. When water freezes into ice, it expands. This splits rocks apart.

Ice can weather rocks in another way. Glaciers are huge masses of ice and snow. They scrape the ground beneath them as they move. This scraping causes many changes.

Erosion

After rock is broken apart by weathering, the pieces often get carried away. This is called **erosion.** Wind, water, glaciers, and gravity all cause erosion.

Water is always causing erosion. Rivers carry away bits of rock and leave them in new places. This forms new islands. Rainwater and ocean waves also cause erosion.

Deserts lack water. Because of this, most desert erosion is caused by wind. Deserts have few plants to block the wind. They also lack plant roots to hold down soil. This means strong winds can cause lots of erosion.

These buttes were eroded by the wind.

Animals are another cause of erosion. Worms, squirrels, and ants all dig holes in the ground. These holes let water and air into the soil. This causes further erosion.

Gravity causes erosion too. Broken rock and other materials often fall down hills as mudflows or rockslides.

Earth is always changing. Most of the time the changes are small and take a long time. Other times the changes are big and happen very fast. Look at the land around you. It may look the same from day to day. But that land is changing all the time!

The Grand Canyon was created by the Colorado River.

Glossary

core   Earth's innermost layer

crust   the outer layer of Earth that is
                made up of different kinds of rock

erosion   the movement of weathered
                material

landform   a solid feature formed on Earth's
                crust

lava   hot, melted rock that comes out of
                a volcano

magma   hot, melted rock beneath Earth's
                surface that is kept under pressure
                by gases

mantle   the thick layer of Earth between the
                crust and the core

weathering any action that breaks rocks into
                smaller pieces